Twenty to **Knit**

Knitted Hats

First published in 2017

Search Press Limited
Wellwood, North Farm Road,
Tunbridge Wells, Kent TN2 3DR

Photography by Paul Bricknell at Search Press Studios. Additional photography on pages 4, 8, 11, 12, 16, 22, 27, 29, 30, 33, 34, 38, 41 and 46 by Fiona Murray.

ISBN: 978-1-78221-453-3

Suppliers
Many of the yarns can be purchased through the author's website: www.theknitknacks.co.uk
If you have difficulty in obtaining any of the materials and equipment mentioned in this book, then please visit the Search Press website for details of suppliers: www.searchpress.com

Printed in China through Asia Pacific Offset

Dedication

To my husband, Trevor, and my sons, Jacob and Matthew, for their ongoing support.

Acknowledgements

I especially appreciate the support from Pete at Rooster Yarns, and Chas and Rachel from UK Alpaca who have enabled me to use a wide range of colours and yarns for the majority of projects in this book. My thanks also go to C & H Fabrics, and Judith from Lady Sew and Sew who supplied the Rowan yarns; Kath from Wensleydale Longwool Sheep Shop; Elaine from Jamieson's of Shetland; and Jayne from Home Farm Wensleydales. Without the help of all these people I would not have had the chance to use such a wide range of natural fibres and colours.

Finally, a huge thanks to Katie French for commissioning this book; to my editor, Beth Harwood; Mary Ellingham and Lin Chan, the publicity team; and the rest of the Search Press team for their invaluable support and encouragement.

Contents

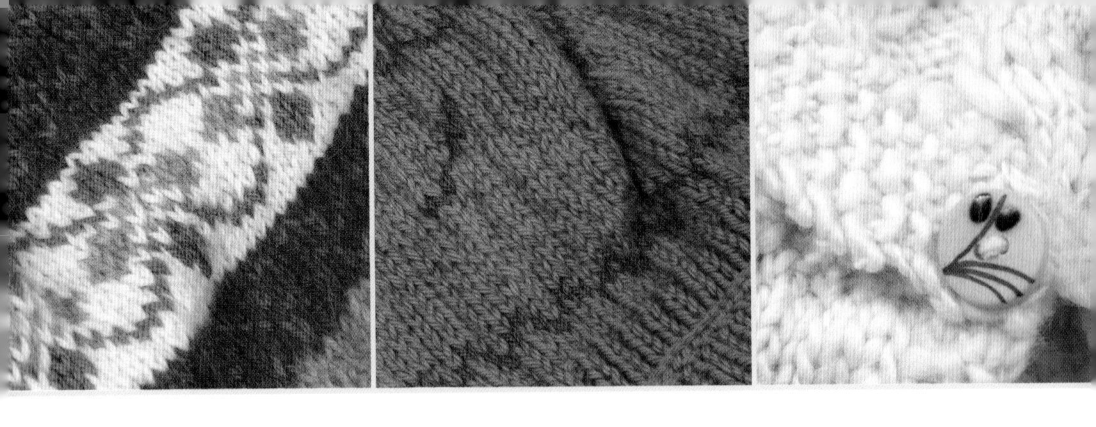

Introduction

Everyone loves a hand-knitted hat in their favourite colour and style. In this book you will find a wide range of patterns covering projects for the new knitter and for the more confident and experienced. The patterns give you the opportunity to knit in the round or on straight needles and the chance to use Fair Isle, cable, lace and textured stitches.

The projects are knitted in a variety of yarns. Colours are interchangeable, allowing scope for creativity. Some patterns can be completed in a day, others are more complex. There are hats for both young and old of both sexes – from trendy teenagers to glamorous grandmothers.

I have really enjoyed playing with the yarns, colours and stitches to produce this collection of designs. I hope you have fun knitting some of the patterns in my book.

Knitting know-how

General notes

These hats will fit an average-sized adult head 53–58cm (21–23in) circumference. Some of the hats are a snug fit and others are more slouchy. If you wish to make them larger or longer you will need additional yarn.

Yarns

Most yarn today comes in ready-prepared balls or skeins. These come in different weights and thicknesses and you can knit directly from them. Other yarn comes in hanks, which are big loops of yarn that are bought by weight and thickness. Before knitting, they need to be wound into a ball so that the yarn does not get knotted as you work.

There is a variety of yarns used in these hat projects and these can be substituted for those of your choice. It is advisable to check the length and weight of yarn that you buy against the ones used in the patterns to ensure that you have enough to finish your projects.

DK (light worsted/8-ply) yarn is a medium thickness yarn that is suitable for many projects. The main light DK (worsted/8-ply) yarn used in these projects is made from alpaca wool, with each ball containing 120m (131yd) of yarn.

Aran (worsted/10-ply) yarn is thicker than light DK (worsted/8-ply) yarn and thus will produce thicker hats.

Bulky (chunky) yarn is thicker still and will produce lovely, snuggly hats, that are ideal for cold weather.

Needles

I have used needles made from sustainable wood for all of these projects. I enjoy knitting with them because of their durability, and they are flexible to work with in all temperatures.

As well as knitting needles, you will also need a blunt-ended needle with a large eye, such as a tapestry needle, for sewing up all your projects and weaving in loose ends.

For some of the projects I have used cable needles. These are also made from sustainable wood and I find that the yarns stay on them better than on metal or plastic ones.

For projects knitted in the round I use circular needles: these are typically 40cm (16in) circulars used in conjunction with DPN in the same size; in other instances I use an 80–100cm (32–40in) circular needle, with the magic loop method.

The crochet chain on the ribbed pompom hat (page 8–9) has been constructed using a crochet hook.

Other materials

For all projects you will need a pair of good-quality, sharp scissors to snip off loose ends of yarn after weaving them into your work.

For some of the hats you will need a pompom maker or two round pieces of card, with circles cut out of the centres, to make a pompom.

For hats worked in the round you will require a stitch marker to mark the start of rows. This will need to be moved up as each row is completed.

Abbreviations

beg beginning
C4B slip next two sts onto cable needle and hold at back, k2 from left-hand needle, k2 from cable needle
C4F slip next two sts onto cable needle and hold at front, k2 from left-hand needle, k2 from cable needle
dec decrease
DPN double-pointed needle(s)
inc increase (by working into the front and back of the same stitch)
k knit
k2tog knit 2 stitches together
kfb knit in front then back of stitch
ktbl knit 1 row through back loop
M1 make 1, pick up the horizontal yarn between the current and the next st, and knit it through back loop
p purl
patt work in pattern as established/instructed
pfb purl in front then back of stitch
psso pass slipped stitch over
p2tog purl 2 stitches together
rem remaining
rep repeat
RS right side/s
s2pp slip 2 sts as if to purl, purl next st, pass 2 slipped sts over
sl slip, usually slip 1 stitch
st(s) stitch(es)
st st stocking stitch (US stockinette stitch)
tbl through back loop
T3B sl 1 st to cable needle and hold at back, k2, p1 from cable needle
T3F sl 2 sts to cable needle and hold at front, p1, k2 from cable needle
WS wrong side/s
yo yarn over
***** repeat the instructions following the * as many times as specified

Yarns and tensions

All the tensions given for the yarns below are the manufacturers' guidelines (except where stated) and for 10 x 10cm (4 x 4in) swatches knitted in stocking stitch: these will be helpful if you decide to use alternative yarns to those given in my patterns.

Home Farm Wensleydales 100% rare breed; Wensleydale and Bluefaced Leicester

Tension over cable pattern: 12 sts x 18 rows using 5.5mm (UK 5, US 9) needles.

Yardage 100g: 86m/96yd.

Hats: Chunky Rainbow Knit.

Aran (worsted/10-ply)

Rowan Cocoon: 80% wool/20% mohair

Tension over moss stitch: 16 sts x 20 rows using 6mm (UK 4, US 10) needles.

Yardage 100g: 115m/126yd.

Hats: Chunky-knit Beanie and Slouchy Hat.

Roosters Aran 50% baby alpaca/50% merino yarn

Tension over stocking stitch with single strand of yarn: 20 sts x 22 rows using 4.5mm (UK 7, US 7) needles.

Yardage 50g: 94m/103yd.

Hats: Cable-knit Bobble (yarn used double), Peruvian-style Hat, Santa Slouch Hat and Winter Walkies.

Wensleydale 100% pure new wool

Tension over stocking stitch: 20 sts x 20 rows using 4.5mm (UK 7, US 7) needles.

Yardage 100g: 160m/174yd.

Hat: Winter Thyme Beanie.

Manos del Uruguay Wool Clasica

Tension over pattern: 15 sts x 24 rows using 5.5mm (UK 5, US 9) needles.

Yardage 100g: 126m/138yd.

Hats: Cable-knit Peaked Cap and Ribbed Pompom Hat.

DK (light worsted/8-ply)

Light DK Yarn

Rowan Felted Tweed, 50% wool/25% alpaca/ 25% viscose

Tension over Fair Isle: 19 sts x 28 rows using 4mm (UK 8, US 6) needles.

Yardage 50g: 175m/191yd.

Hats: Green Patterned Cap and Lacy Rose Beret.

UK Alpaca: Superfine Alpaca – 70% alpaca/30% Bluefaced Leicester

Tension over st st and single ply yarn 20 sts x 29 rows using 4mm (UK 8, US 6) needles.

Yardage 50g: 112m/123yd per ball.

Hats: Autumnal Beanie (yarn used double), Fair Isle Tam, Striped Lilac Cap and Sunday Stroll.

Manos del Uruguay: Silk Blend – 30% silk/70% extra-fine merino

Tension: 20 sts x 30 rows using 4mm (UK 8, US 6) needles

Yardage 50g: 135m/148yd.

Hat: Heather Beret.

4-ply (Fingering)

UK Alpaca: 80% baby alpaca/20% Tussah Silk

Tension over Fair Isle: 35 sts x 40 rows using 3.25mm (UK 10, US 3) needles

Yardage 50g: 225m/246yd.

Hat: Fair Isle Beanie.

Roosters: Baby Rooster superwash merino yarn

Tension over st st: 23 sts and 36 rows using 3.25mm (UK 10/US 3) circular needles

Yardage 50g: 125m/137yd.

Hat: Cloche.

Jamieson's Shetland Spindrift

Tension over Fair Isle: 28 sts x 30 rows using 3mm (UK 11, US 2½) needles.

Yardage 25g: 105m/114yd.

Hat: Striped-rim Fair Isle.

Ribbed Pompom Hat

Materials:

1 ball of Aran (worsted/10-ply) variegated yarn; 100g/126m/138yd

Small amount of gold yarn in similar thickness for pompoms

Needles:

5.5mm (UK 5, US 9) circular needles, 40cm (16in) long

5.5mm (UK 5, US 9) crochet hook (optional for chain)

Tension:

Tension over rib: 15 sts x 24 rows using 5.5mm (UK 5, US 9) needles

Instructions:

Using the circular needles, cast on 85 sts. Place a stitch marker, to denote start of each round. Join the round being careful not to twist any stitches. Slip marker as you pass it at the end of each round.

All rounds: *k3, p2, rep from * to end.

Continue working rounds as above until work measures 18cm (7in).

Shaping the crown

Next round (dec): *k3, p2tog, rep from * to end [68 sts].

Next 3 rounds: *k3, p1, rep from * to end.

Next round (dec): *k1, k2tog, p1, rep from * to end [51 sts].

Next round: *k2tog, yo, p1.

Next 9 rounds: *k2, p1, rep from * to end.

Next round: *k1, M1, rep from * to end [102 sts].

Next round: Knit.

Next row: Cast off.

Making up

Using four strands of yarn, make 1 x 25cm (10in) crochet chain or a chain using loops to thread through spaces in the crown of the hat.

Make two pompoms in your contrasting yarn (or the same colour if you prefer).

Attach one pompom to each end of the chain once it has been threaded though the hat.

Weave all loose ends into rear of work. Draw hat closed and tie knot in chain to secure.

Winter Thyme Beanie

Materials:

3 balls of Aran (worsted/10-ply) 100% pure wool in storm grey (A), lime sherbet (B), purple thyme (C); 100g/160m/174yd

Needles:

4.5mm (UK 7, US 7) needles

Tension:

Tension over st st: 20 sts x 22 rows using 4.5mm (UK 7, US 7) needles

Instructions:

Bottom band

Using yarn A, cast on 14 sts.

Foundation row: Knit each st through back loop to form a neat edge.

Row 1 (WS): using yarn B, purl.

Row 2 (RS): using yarn B, knit.

Rows 3 and 4: using yarn A knit.

Row 5: using yarn C, purl.

Row 6: using yarn C, knit.

Rows 7 and 8: using yarn A, knit.

Row 9: using yarn B, purl.

Row 10: using yarn B, knit.

Rows 11 and 12: using yarn A, knit.

Rows 13–24: as rows 1–12.

Rows 25–28: as rows 5–8.

Rows 29–32: as rows 1–4.

Rows 33–36: as rows 9–12.

Rows 37–40: as rows 5–8.

Rows 41 and 42: as rows 1 and 2.

Continue repeating rows 3–42 until band measures 56cm (22in).

Cast off sts.

Main body

Fold band in half lengthwise, with WS together.

With RS facing and yarn C, pick up and knit 97 sts across the top edge of folded band ensuring that sts are picked up from the front and the back in each stitch (this joins the band).

Next row: using yarn C, knit.

Cut off yarn C.

Rows 1–4: work four rows in st st using yarn A.

Row 5: k15A, k3B, k17A, k3B, k14A, k3B, k15A, k3B, k15A, k3B, k6A.

Row 6: p5A, p7B, p11A, p7B, p11A, p7B, p10A, p7B, p11A, p7B, p14A.

Row 7: k15A, k8B, k7A, k8B, k9A, k8B, k10A, k8B, k10A, k8B, k6A.

Row 8: p6A, p9B, p9A, p9B, p9A, p9B, p8A, p9B, p5A, p9B, p15A.

Row 9: k16A, k8B, k5A, k8B, k9A, k8B, k10A, k8B, k10A, k8B, k7A.

Row 10: p8A, p8B, p10A, p8B, p10A, p8B, p9A, p8B, p3A, p8B, p17A.

Row 11: k18A, k7B, k3A, k7B, k10A, k7B, k11A, k7B, k11A, k7B, k9A.

Row 12: p10A, p6B, p12A, p6B, p12A, p6B, p11A, p6B, p3A, p6B, p6A, p5B, p8A.

Row 13: k6A, k10B, k5A, k4B, k3A, k4B, k13A, k4B, k14A, k4B, k14A, k4B, k12A.

Row 14: p15A, p1B, p17A, p1B, p17A, p1B, p16A, p1B, p3A, p1B, p7A, p12B, p5A.

Row 15: k4A, k14B, k7A, k1B, k1A, k1B, k16A, k1B, k17A, k1B, k17A, k1B, k16A.

Cut off yarn A.

Row 16: p16C, p1B, p17C, p1B, p16C, p1B, p18C, p1B, p1C, p1B, p7C, p15B, p3C.

Cut off yarn C.

Row 17: as row 15.

Row 18: as row 14.

Row 19: as row 13.

Row 20: as row 12.

Row 21: as row 11.

Row 22: as row 10.

Row 23: as row 9.

Row 24: as row 8.

Row 25: as row 7.

Row 26: as row 6.

Row 27: as row 5.

Cut off yarn B.

Continue hat using yarn A only.

Row 28: purl, decreasing 1 st in middle of row [96 sts].

Decreasing for crown

Row 29: *k10, k2tog, rep from * to end [88 sts].

Row 30: Purl.

Row 31: *k9, k2tog, rep from * to end [80 sts].

Row 32: Purl.

Row 33: *k8, k2tog, rep from * to end [72 sts].

Row 34: Purl.

Row 35: *k7, k2tog, rep from * to end [64 sts].

Row 36: Purl.

Row 37: *k6, k2tog, rep from * to end [56 sts].

Row 38: Purl.

Row 39: *k5, k2tog, rep from * to end [48 sts].

Row 40: Purl.

Row 41: *k4, k2tog, rep from * to end [40 sts].

Row 42: Purl.

Row 43: *k3, k2tog, rep from * to end [32 sts].

Row 44: Purl.

Row 45: *k2, k2tog, rep from * to end [24 sts].

Row 46: Purl.

Row 47: *k1, k2tog, rep from * to end [16 sts].

Row 48: Purl.

Cut yarn and thread through rem sts.

Making up

Pull yarn up tightly and fasten off securely. Join back seam using mattress stitch.

Chunky-knit Beanie

Materials:

1 ball of Aran (worsted/10-ply) in chunky wool or mohair in teal; 100g/115m/126yd

Needles:

1 pair of 6mm (UK 4, US 10) needles

1 cable needle

Tension:

Tension over moss stitch: 16 sts x 20 rows using 6mm (UK 4, US 10) needles

Tension over double moss stitch: 14 sts x 20 rows

Instructions:

Note: Pattern uses moss stitch and double moss stitch.

Cable band

Cast on 16 sts.

Foundation row: Knit each st through back loop to form a neat edge

Row 1 (RS): knit.

Row 2: Purl.

Rows 3 and 4: as rows 1 and 2.

Row 5: C14B, k2.

Row 6: Purl.

Rows 7 and 8: as rows 1 and 2.

These 8 rows form the pattern for the band.

Repeat rows 1–8 until band measures approx. 60cm (23½in), ending with row 8.

Cast off sts leaving last st on your needle.

Main body

With RS facing, pick up and knit 75 sts along the straight edge of the cable band.

Row 1 (WS): *k2, p2, rep from * to last 3 sts, k2, p1.

Row 2 (RS): p1, k2, *p2, k2, rep from * to end.

Continue working in double moss stitch until work measures approx. 13cm (5in) with RS facing for next row.

Now work in single moss stitch and at the same time decrease for the crown as follows:

Row 1: *moss st 6, work 3 tog, moss st 6, rep from * to end [65 sts].

Rows 2–4: work 3 rows single moss st.

Row 5: *moss st 5, work 3 tog, moss st 5, rep from * to end [55 sts].

Row 6 and all even-numbered rows to row 14: single moss st.

Row 7: *moss st 4, work 3 tog, moss st 4, rep from * to end [45 sts].

Row 9: *moss st 3, work 3 tog, moss st 3, rep from * to end [35 sts].

Row 11: *moss st 2, work 3 tog, moss st 2, rep from * to end [25 sts].

Row 13: *moss st 1, work 3 tog, moss st 1, rep from * to end [15 sts].

Row 15: *work 3 sts tog, rep from * to end.

Making up

Cut yarn and thread through remaining stitches. Pull yarn up tightly and fasten off securely. Join back seam using mattress stitch.

Striped Lilac Cap

Materials:

3 balls of light DK (worsted/8-ply) alpaca yarn in black (A), lilac (B), damson (C); 50g/112m/122yd

Needles:

1 pair of 4mm (UK 8, US 6) needles

5 x 4mm DPN (UK 8, US 6)

4mm (UK 8, US 6) circular needle, 40cm (16in)

Tension:

Tension over textured pattern: 28 sts x 30 rows using 4mm (UK 8, US 6) needles

Instructions:

Please check tension carefully before starting the hat.

Using 4mm (UK 8, US 6) single-pointed knitting needles and yarn A cast on 25 sts.

Note: When changing colours twist the yarns regularly at the same edge to avoid large loops.

Rows 1 and 2: Knit.

Row 3 (RS): p1, *k1,p1, rep from * to end.

Row 4: k1, *p1, k1, rep from * to end.

Repeat rows 1–4 using yarn B.

Repeat rows 1–4 using yarn C.

Continue the 12-row pattern sequence until work measures approx. 48cm (19in), ending with row 12. Before casting off, check the hat fits snugly and adjust length as necessary.

Cast off.

Top of hat

Cast on 8 sts with 4mm (UK 8, US 6) DPN and yarn A.

Distribute sts evenly across the 4 needles and place a st marker to denote start of round.

Round 1: *kfb, rep from * to end [16 sts].

Round 2: Knit.

Round 3: *kfb, k1, rep from * to end [24 sts].

Round 4: Knit.

Round 5: *kfb, k2, rep from * to end [32 sts].

Round 6: Knit.

Round 7: *kfb, k3, rep from * to end [40 sts].

Round 8: Knit.

Round 9: *kfb, k4, rep from * to end [48 sts].

Round 10: Knit.

Round 11: *kfb, k5, rep from * to end [56 sts].

Round 12: Knit.

Round 13: *kfb, k6, rep from * to end [64 sts].

Rounds 14 and 15: Knit.

Round 16: *kfb, k7, rep from * to end [72 sts].

Rounds 17 and 18: Knit.

Round 19: *kfb, k8, rep from * to end [80 sts].

Rounds 20 and 21: Knit.

Round 22: *kfb, k9, rep from * to end [88 sts].

Rounds 23 and 24: Knit.

Round 25: *kfb, k10, rep from * to end [96 sts].

Round 26: *k48, kfb, k47 [97 sts].

Rounds 27 and 28: Purl.

Rounds 29 and 30: p1, *k1, p1, rep from * to end.

Repeat rounds 27–30, once more.

Knit 1 one row.

Cast off.

Making up

Join cast on and cast off ends of band together using mattress stitch with RS facing. Mark the centre of the band (opposite the seamed edge) with a pin. Fold the top of the hat in half and place markers to note half of the circumference. (These markers will allow you to fit the pieces together more easily.) With RS facing, join the top of the hat to the bottom band (the edge where you have carried up the colours) matching the marked points and easing your work so that it fits perfectly.

Weave in all loose ends.

Heather Beret

Materials:

2 balls of light DK (worsted/8-ply) silk/extra fine merino yarn in olive oil (A), variegated yarn (B); 50g/135m/148yd

Needles:

1 pair of 4mm (UK 8, US 6) needles

1 pair of 4.5mm (UK 7, US 7) needles

Tension:

Tension over st st: 20 sts x 32 rows using 4.5mm (UK 7, US 7) needles

Instructions:

Using yarn A and 4mm needles cast on 100 sts.

Foundation row: knit each st through back loop to form a neat edge.

Rows 1–4: using yarn B, *ktbl, p1, rep from * to end.

Rows 5 and 6: using yarn A, *ktbl, p1, rep from * to end.

Row 7: using yarn B, *ktbl, p1, rep from * to end.

Row 8: using yarn B, *ktbl, p1, rep from * to end decreasing 1 st in the middle of the row [99 sts].

Row 9: using yarn B, *k3, inc 1, k4, inc1, rep from * to last st, k1 [127 sts].

Row 10: using yarn B, purl.

Now work pattern as outlined below, keeping the stripes as follows: 2 rows yarn A, 4 rows yarn B.

Rows 11–18: work 8 rows in st st.

Row 19: *k8, inc 1, rep from * to last 7 sts, k7 [142 sts].

Row 20: Purl.

Rows 21–34: work 14 rows in st st.

Row 35: *k8, sl 1, k1, psso, rep from * to last 2 sts, k2 [128 sts].

Row 36: Purl.

Rows 37–42: work 6 rows in st st.

Row 43: *k7, sl 1, k1, psso, rep from * to last 2 sts, k2 [114 sts].

Row 44: Purl.

Rows 45 and 46: work 2 rows in st st.

Row 47: *k6, sl 1, k1, psso, rep from * to last 2 sts, k2 [100 sts].

Row 48: Purl.

Row 49: *k5, sl 1, k1, psso, rep from * to last 2 sts, k2 [86 sts].

Row 50: Purl.

Rows 51 and 52: work 2 rows in st st.

Row 53: *k4, sl 1, k1, psso, rep from * to last 2 sts, k2 [72 sts].

Row 54: Purl.

Row 55: *k3, sl 1, k1, psso, rep from * to last 2 sts, k2 [58 sts].

Row 56: Purl

Row 57: *k2, sl 1, k1, psso, rep from * to last 2 sts, k2 [44 sts].

Row 58: Purl.

Row 59: *k2tog, rep to end [22 sts].

Making up

Cut yarn and thread through remaining stitches. Pull yarn up tightly and fasten off securely. Join back seam using mattress stitch.

Cable-knit Peaked Cap

Materials:

1 ball of Aran (worsted/10-ply) pure wool in cream; 100g/126m/138yd

Stitch marker

Piece of plastic for peak

2 buttons

Needles:

5mm (UK 6, US 8) circular needles, 40cm (16in) long

1 set 5mm (UK 6, US 8) DPN

1 cable needle

Tension:

Tension over cable pattern: 22 sts x 22 rows using 5mm (UK 6, US 8) needles

Instructions:

Main body

Using the circular needles, cast on 96 sts. Place a stitch marker, to denote start of each round. Join the round being careful not to twist any stitches. Slip marker as you pass it on each round.

Round 1: *k1, p1, rep from * to end.

Round 2: *p1, k1, rep from * to end.

Round 3: *k1, p1, rep from * to end.

Start cable pattern as follows:

Round 1: *k12, p4, rep from * to end.

Round 2: as round 1.

Round 3: *C6F, C6B, p4, rep from * to end.

Rounds 4–8: as round 2.

Repeat rounds 1–8 until work measures approx. 17cm (6¾in) ending with a round 4.

Shaping the crown

Round 1: *k2tog 6 times, p2tog two times, rep from * to end [48 sts].

Change to DPN. Distribute remaining sts over 3 needles placing your marker at the start of every round.

Round 2: *k2tog 3 times, p2tog once, rep from * to end [24 sts].

Rounds 3 and 4: *k3, p1 rep from * to end.

Round 5: *k2tog, k1, p1, rep from * to end [18 sts].

Making up

Cut yarn and thread through rem sts. Pull yarn up tightly and fasten off. Weave in all loose ends.

Peak

Using straight needles, cast on 40 sts.

Row 1 (RS): knit 25, turn.

Row 2: slip 1, p12, turn.

Row 3: slip 1, k15, turn.

Row 4: slip 1, p18, turn.

Continue in pattern as set increasing 3 sts every row before the turn, until all 40 sts have been worked.

Work 6 rows in st st.

Cast off 2 sts at the beg of next 10 rows [20 sts].

Cast off 3 sts at the beg of next 4 rows [8 sts].

Cast off rem 8 sts.

Press the peak and fold it in half. Cut a piece of plastic to the shape of the peak (I used the top of a plastic biscuit box) and place inside the peak. Sew the edges of the peak together with RS facing.

Strap

Cast on 7 sts.

Row 1: *k1, p1 rep from * to last st, k1.

Repeat row 1 until work measures approx. 25cm (10in).

Cast off.

Making up

Sew the peak to the centre front of the cap, using the cables to help you to centre it. Sew the strap at either end of the peak and place and sew a button at either end of the strap.

Weave in all loose ends.

Lacy Rose Beret

Materials:

1 ball of DK (light worsted/8-ply) in pale pink; 50g/175m/191yd

Stitch marker

1 button (optional)

Needles:

1 pair of 3.75mm (UK 9, US 5) needles

4.5mm (UK 7, US 7) circular needle, 40cm (16in) long

4 x 4.5mm (UK 7, US 7) DPN

1 cable needle

Tension:

Tension over lace pattern: 18 sts x 30 rows using 4.5mm (UK 7, US 7) single-pointed needles

Instructions:

Please check tension carefully before starting the hat.

Using 3.75mm (UK 9, US 5) needles, cast on 118 sts.

Row 1 (RS): *k2, C4F, rep from * to last 4 sts, k4.

Row 2: Purl.

Row 3: Knit.

Row 4: Purl.

Rows 5 and 6: as rows 1 and 2.

Row 7: *C4B, k2 rep from * to last 4 sts, C4B.

Row 8: Purl.

Knit sts onto a 4.5mm circular needle increasing 2 sts evenly across the row [120 sts].

Join to work in the round and place a stitch marker to denote start of each round. Slip marker as you pass it on each round.

Round 1: *k4, yo, k1, sl 1, k1, psso k3, rep from * to end of round.

Round 2: *k2, k2togtbl, k1, yo, k5, rep from * to end of round.

Round 3: *k6, yo, k1, sl 1, k1, psso, k1, rep from * to end of round.

Round 4: *k2togtbl, k1, yo, k7, rep from * to end of round.

Round 5: *k3, k2tog, k1, yo, k4, rep from * to end of round.

Round 6: *k5, yo, k1, k2tog, k2, rep from * to end of round.

Round 7: *k1, k2tog, k1, yo, k6, rep from * to end of round.

Round 8: *k7, yo, k1, k2tog, rep from * to end of round.

Repeat rows 1–8 twice more and then rows 1–4 once more.

Decreasing for crown

Change to DPN when yarn becomes tight on circular needles.

Round 1: *k5, sk2po (slip one st, knit 2 stitches together, pass slipped st over the knitted st), k4, rep from * to end of round [100 sts].

Round 2: Knit.

Round 3: *k4, sk2po, k3, rep from * to end of round [80 sts].

Round 4: Knit.

Round 5: *k3, sk2po, k2, rep from * to end of round [60 sts].

Round 6: *k2, sk2po, k1, rep from * to end of round [40 sts].

Round 7: *k1, sk2po, rep from * to end of round [20 sts].

Round 8: *k1, sk2po, k1, rep from * to end of round [16 sts].

Cut yarn, leaving a long tail.

Making up

Pull yarn up tightly and fasten off securely. Join border seam using mattress stitch

Optional: Sew button onto where the seams are joined as the bottom of the hat.

Cloche

Materials:

2 balls of 4-ply (fingering) merino in gooseberry (A); 50g/125m/137yd

Small amount of 4-ply (fingering) merino in grey (B)

1 button for the centre of the flower

Needles:

1 set 3.25mm (UK 10, US 3) DPN

1 pair of 3mm (UK 11, US 2½) needles

3.25mm (UK 10, US 3) circular needle, 40cm (16in) long

3mm (UK 11, US 2½) circular needle, 40cm (16in) long

Tension:

Tension over st st: 23 sts x 36 rows using 3.25mm (UK 10, US 3) circular needles

Instructions:

Using 3.25mm (UK 10, US 3) DPN and yarn A, cast on 8 sts. Divide the sts over the 4 needles. place a stitch marker to denote start of each round. Join the round, being careful not to twist any stitches. Slip marker as you pass it.

Round 1: kfb into each st to end [16 sts].

Round 2 and every even-numbered round: Knit.

Round 3: *k2, yo, rep from * to end [24 sts].

Round 5: *k3, yo, rep from * to end [32 sts].

Round 7: *k4, yo, rep from * to end [40 sts].

Round 9: *k5, yo, rep from * to end [48 sts].

Continue to increase every other round (increasing 8 sts per inc round) until there are 120 sts on needles [30 sts per needle].

Transfer sts to 3.25mm (UK 10, US 3) circular needle maintaining beginning of round marker placement and place 1 locking stitch marker on this row to use for height measurement.

Work in st st (knitting every row) until work measures 8cm (3¼in) from marker.

Change to 3mm (UK 11, US 2½) circular needle.

Commence 1 x 1 moss st as follows:

Round 1: *k1, p1, rep from * to end.

Repeat round 1 until moss st section measures 3cm (1¼in).

Brim

Change back to 3.25mm (UK 10, US 3) circular needle.

Work 2 rounds in garter st (knit 1 round, purl 1 round].

Round 3: *p15, m1, rep from * to end [128 sts].

Round 4: Purl.

Round 5: *p16, m1, rep from * to end [136 sts].

Round 6: Purl.

Round 7: p102, turn leaving rem 34 sts unworked.

Round 8: p68, turn, leaving rem 34 sts unworked.

Ear flap

Round 1: p64, turn.

Round 2: p60, turn.

Continue as above, working 4 fewer sts across each row until you have 36 sts ending on a WS row.

Next row: p19, turn.

Next row: p2, turn.

Next row: p4, turn.

Next row: p6, turn.

Continue as above, working 2 more sts per row until the row p32 turn has been worked.

Next row: p35, turn.

Knit to original marker and then knit 3 rounds more.

Cast off loosely.

Flower

Using 3mm (UK 11, US 2½) straight needles cast on 8 sts with yarn B.

Row 1: knit each st through back loop.

Row 2: Knit.

Row 3: kfb, k to end [9 sts].

Row 4: Knit.

Row 5: kfb, k to end [10 sts].

Row 6: Knit.

Row 7: kfb, k to end [11 sts].

Row 8: Knit.

Row 9: k2tog, k to end [10 sts].

Row 10: Knit.

Row 11: k2tog, k to end [9 sts].

Row 12: Knit.

Row 13: k2tog, k to end [8 sts]

Row 14: Knit.

Row 15: cast off 5, knit to end [3 sts].

Row 16: knit 3, cast on 5 [8 sts].

Rep rows 1–16 three more times and then rows 1–14 once.

Cast off sts and cut yarn.

Flower centre

Using yarn A, cast on 6 sts.

Row 1: cast off 5 sts.

Row 2: cast on 5 sts.

Repeat rows 1 and 2 seven more times.

Cast off sts.

Making up

Join the two ends of the large flower by stitching the bottom of the end petals together. Using a running stitch run your thread along the bottom edges of the petals. Draw the stitches together to gather them up. Stitch the flower centre into the middle of the flower. Place your button in the centre of the flower and sew the complete flower onto the ear flap.

Sew in all loose ends.

Autumnal Beanie

Materials:

2 balls of DK (light worsted/8-ply) alpaca yarn in chocolate; 50g/112m/123yd

Stitch marker

Needles:

4.5mm (UK 7, US 7) circular needle, 40cm (16in) long

4 x 4.5mm (UK 7, US 7) DPN

Tension:

Tension over st st with yarn used double: 20 sts x 22 rows using 4.5mm (UK 7, US 7) needles

Instructions:

Note: Yarn is used double throughout.

Cast on 80 sts. Place a stitch marker to denote the start of each round. Join the round, being careful not to twist any stitches. Slip marker as you pass it on each round.

Rounds 1–8: Purl.

Rounds 9 and 10: *k1, p1, rep from * to end of round.

Work in st st (knit every round) until st st section measures 12.5cm (5in).

Shaping crown

Round 1: *k8, k2tog, rep from * to end of round [72 sts].

Round 2: Knit.

Round 3: *k7, k2tog, rep from * to end of round [64 sts].

Round 4: Knit.

Round 5: *k6, k2tog, rep from * to end of round [56 sts].

Round 6: knit

Round 7: *k5, k2tog, rep from * to end [48 sts].

Round 8: Knit.

Change to DPN, distributing the sts evenly across 3 needles.

Round 9: *k4, k2tog, rep from * to end of round [40 sts].

Round 10: Knit.

Round 11: *k3, k2tog, rep from * to end of round [32 sts].

Round 12: Knit.

Round 13: *k2, k2tog, rep from * to end of round [24 sts].

Round 14: *k1, k2tog, rep from * to end of round [16 sts].

Making up

Cut yarn and thread through remaining stitches. Pull yarn up tightly and fasten off. Weave in all loose ends. If you weave your ends in neatly, the hat can also be worn with the purl side out for a slightly different look.

Santa Slouch Hat

Materials:

2 balls of Aran (worsted/10-ply) alpaca/merino blend in rooster; 50g/94m/103yd

1 ball of Aran (worsted/10-ply) alpaca/merino blend in cream; 50g/94m/103yd

Stitch marker

Needles:

1 set of 5mm (UK 6, US 8) DPN

5mm (UK 6, US 8) circular needle, 40cm (16in) long

Tension:

Tension over st st: 18 sts x 24 rows using 5mm (UK 6, US 8) circular needles

Instructions:

Using 5mm (UK 6, US 8) circular needles and yarn A cast on 87 sts and place a stitch marker to denote start of each round. Join the round being careful not to twist any stitches. Slip marker as you pass it on each round.

Rounds 1–9: purl, using yarn A.

Cut off yarn A and continue in yarn B.

Knit every round until work measures 14cm (5½in).

Decreasing for crown

Next round: *k27, sl 1, k1, psso, rep from * to end [84 sts].

Next 2 rounds: Knit.

Next round: *k26, sl 1, k1, psso, rep from * to end [81 sts].

Next 2 rounds: Knit.

Continue decreasing as above (3 sts on every decrease row) until you find it hard to work on circular needles.

Change to DPN, dividing your sts evenly across them and continue decreasing as above on every third row until you have 6 sts remaining.

Cut yarn and, using a needle, thread it through rem sts to draw them up tightly and fasten off.

Making up

Using yarn A, make a large pompom. Sew the pompom at the tip of the cast-off end.

Version B, striped

Work as A in chosen colours and stripes of either 8 or 10 rows until you have 6 sts remaining.

Optional: Make 3 i-cords. Using 5mm (UK 6, US 8) DPN, arrange 3 sts on each needle and work each i-cord separately as follows: *knit 3 sts, slide to other end of needle without turning work; rep from * until 14 rows have been worked.

Cast off sts. Repeat for remaining i-cords.

Weave in all loose ends.

Winter Walkies

Materials:

3 balls of Aran (worsted/10-ply) alpaca/merino blend in ocean (A), rooster (B), mushroom (C); 50g/94m/103yd

Needles:

1 pair of 4.5mm (UK 7, US 7) needles

1 pair of 5mm (UK 6, US 8) needles

Tension:

Tension over pattern: 20 sts x 22 rows using 5mm (UK 6, US 8) needles

Instructions:

Using 4.5mm (UK 7, US 7) needles and yarn A, cast on 102 sts.

Foundation row: knit each st through back loop to form a neat edge.

Rows 1–26: *k1, p1, rep from * to end of row

Change to 5mm (UK 6, US 8) needles.

Row 27 and 28: using yarn A, work 2 rows in st st.

Chart A

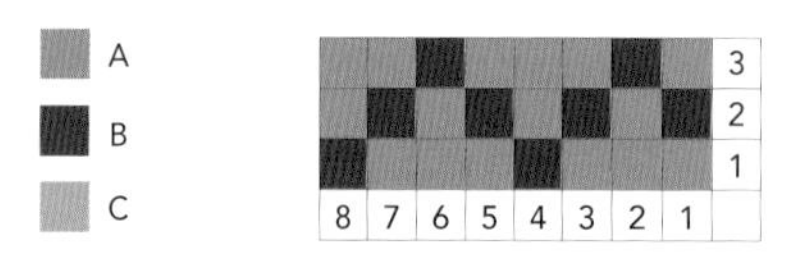

Note: When working Fair Isle the odd-numbered rows are read from right to left (knit rows) and for even-numbered rows the chart is read from left to right (purl rows).

Row 29–31: Work from chart A, repeating the pattern twelve times and then the first 6 sts once. On the second row the pattern starts on stitch 6, working back to stitch 1, then repeat the full pattern to end.

Row 32: purl yarn A.

Chart B

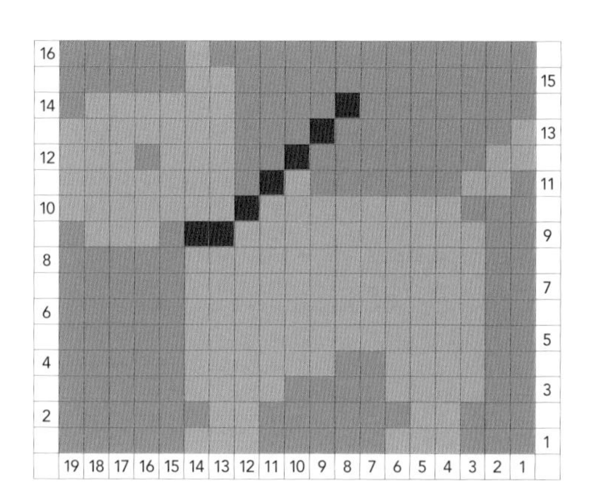

Rows 33–48: work from chart B, setting spacing as follows: k1A *work sts 1–19 from chart, k1A, rep from * to last st, k1A.

Rows 49 and 50: using yarn A, work 2 rows in st st.

Rows 51–53: as rows 29–31.

Rows 54–56: work in st st starting with a purl row.

Cut off yarn A.

Shaping the crown

Row 57: using yarn B *k2tog, rep from * to end [51 sts].

Row 58: Purl.

Row 59: k1, *k2tog, rep from * to end [26 sts].

Row 60: Purl.

Making up

Cut yarn and thread through remaining stitches. Pull yarn up tightly and fasten off securely. Join back seam using mattress stitch.

Sunday Stroll

Materials:

5 balls of light DK (worsted/8-ply) alpaca yarn in brown (A), green (B), sandstone (C), rust (D), mustard (E); 50g/112m/191yd

Needles:

1 pair of 4mm (UK 8, US 6) needles

1 pair of 4.5mm (UK 7, US 7) needles

Tension:

Tension over Fair Isle pattern: 24 sts x 24 rows using 4.5mm (UK 7, US 7) needles.

Instructions:

Please check tension carefully before starting the hat.

Using 4mm (UK 8, US 6) needles and yarn A, cast on 100 sts.

Foundation row: knit each st through back loop to form a neat edge.

Rib rows 1 and 2: using yarn B, *k1, p1, rep from * to end.

Rib row 3: using yarn A, *k1, p1, rep from * to end.

Rib rows 4 and 5: using yarn C, *k1, p1, rep from * to end.

Rib row 6: using yarn A, *k1, p1, rep from * to end.

Rib rows 7 and 8: using yarn D *k1, p1, rep from * to end.

Rib row 9: using yarn `A *k1, p1, rep from * to end.

Rib rows 10 and 11: using yarn E *k1, p1, rep from * to end.

Rib row 12: using yarn A *k1, p1, rep from * to end.

Rib rows 13 and 14: using yarn B *k1, p1, rep from * to end

Main body

Change to 4.5mm (UK 7, US 7) needles.

Next row (RS): using yarn A *k3, kfb, rep from * to end [125 sts].

Next row (WS): using yarn A, purl increasing 3 sts evenly across the row [128 sts].

Now work rows 1–24 from the chart, stranding yarn loosely on the WS of work to get the correct tension.

Next, repeat rows 9–14 using D instead of E.

Now work 2 rows st st using yarn A.

Decreasing for crown

Row 1: *k1A, k2togA, k3E, k2A, rep from * to end [112 sts].

Row 2: *p1A, p5E, p1A, rep from * to end.

Row 3: k1A, *k2E, k1B, k2E, k2togA, rep from * to end finiching with k1A instead of k2togA [97 sts].

Row 4: p2A, p3E, *p3A, p3E, rep from * to last 2 sts, p2A.

Row 5: *k2Atog, k3A, rep from * to last 2 sts, k2Atog [77 sts].

Row 6: purl using yarn A.

From now on the hat is completed in A only.

Row 7: *k2, k2tog, rep from * to last st, k1 [58 sts].

Row 8: Purl.

Row 9: *k1, k2tog, rep from * to last st, k1 [39 sts].

Row 10: Purl.

Row 11: *k2tog, rep from * to last st, k1 [20 sts].

Making up

Cut yarn and thread through remaining stitches. Pull yarn up tightly and fasten off securely. Join back seam using mattress stitch.

Chart

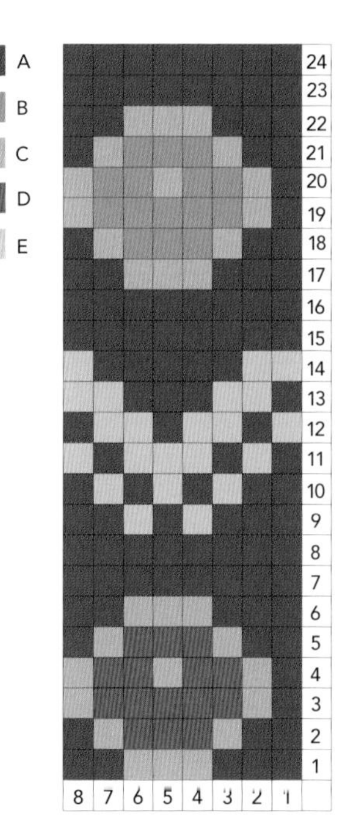

Left, an alternative colour scheme for the Sunday Stroll hat.

Green Patterned Cap

Materials:

5 balls of light DK (worsted/8-ply) yarn in light green (A), rust (B), dark grey (C), mauve (D), yellow (E); 50g/175m/191yd

Needles:

1 pair of 4mm (UK 8, US 6) needles

Large-eyed tapestry needle

Tension:

Tension over Fair Isle: 19 sts x 28 rows using 4mm (UK 8, US 6) needles

Instructions:

Main body

Using 4mm (UK 8, US 6) needles and yarn C, cast on 124 sts.

Rows 1–9: *k2, p2, rep from * to end.

Next 2 rows: knit (these rows will form fold line).

Start working from the chart below:

Chart

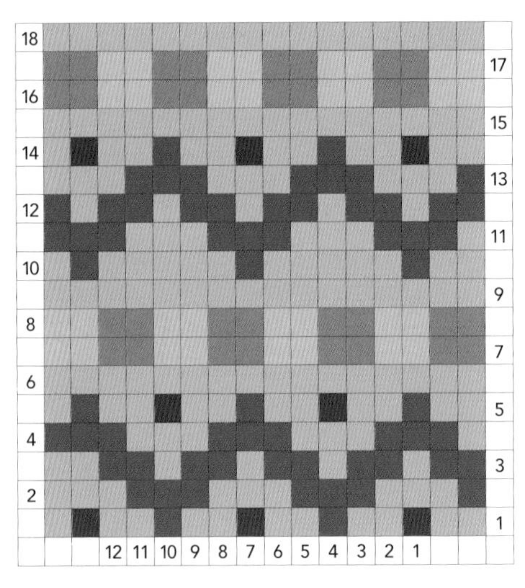

Work 2 edge stitches, then repeat 12-stitch pattern ten times, followed by the 2 remaining edge stitches, noting that all odd-numbered rows are knit reading the chart from right to left, and all even-numbered rows are purled reading chart from left to right. Remember to twist the yarn each time you change colour. Work the 18-row pattern from the chart twice to form the body of the hat. Cast off sts.

Top

When working the top, work first row in yarn A, then alternate between yarns B and A, working in 6-row stripes and finishing with yarn A on last row.

Cast on 16 sts using yarn A.

Row 1: kfb, k to last st, kfb [18 sts].

Row 2: pfb 3 times, p to last 3 sts, pfb 3 times [24 sts].

Row 3: kfb, k to last st, kfb [26 sts].

Row 4: pfb twice, p to last 2 sts, pfb twice [30 sts].

Row 5: kfb, k to last st, kfb [32 sts].

Row 6: pfb, k to last st, pfb [34 sts].

Row 7: kfb, k to last st, kfb [36 sts].

Row 8: Purl.

Row 9: kfb, k to last st, kfb [38 sts].

Row 10: Purl.

Rows 11 and 12: as rows 5 and 6 [42 sts].

Rows 13–32: work in st st for 10 rows.

Row 33: ssk (slip 1 st knitwise, slip next st knitwise, insert left needle into front of both sts, knit together through back loop), k to last 2 sts, k2tog [40 sts].

Row 34: Purl.

Rows 35 and 36: as rows 33 and 34 [38 sts].

Row 37: ssk, k to last 2 sts, k2tog [36 sts].

Row 38: p2tog, p to last 2 sts, p2tog [34 sts].

Rows 39 and 40: as rows 37 and 38 [30 sts].

Row 41: ssk twice, k to last 4 sts, k2tog twice [26 sts].

Row 42: p2tog, p to last 2 sts, p2tog [24 sts].

Row 43: ssk 3 times, k to last 6 sts, k2tog 3 times [18 sts].

Row 44: p2tog, p to last 2 sts, p2tog [16 sts].

Cast off.

Making up

With RS facing, join the top of the brim to the top of the hat easing your work as you sew. Using mattress stitch and RS facing, join the side seams. Turn the ribbing to the WS of the hat and sew into place using slip stitch.

Weave in all loose ends.

Slouchy Hat

Materials:

2 balls of Aran (worsted/10-ply) wool/mohair blend in seascape teal (A), mountain grey (B); 100g/115m/126yd

Needles:

7mm (UK 2, US 10½) circular needles, 40cm (16in) long

7mm (UK 2, US 10½) DPN

Tension:

Tension over st st:14 sts x 18 rows using 7mm (UK 2, US 10½) circular needles

Instructions:

With 7mm (UK 2, US 10½) circular needles and yarn A, cast on 65 sts. Place a stitch marker to denote start of each round. Join the round, being careful not to twist any stitches. Slip marker as you pass it on each round.

Using yarn A:

Round 1: Knit.

Round 2: Purl.

Repeat rounds 1 and 2 four more times, then repeat round 1 only once.

Change to yarn B.

Rounds 13–22: Knit.

Change to yarn A.

Rounds 23, 25, 27, 29: Knit.

Rounds 24, 26, 28, 30: Purl.

Repeat rounds 13–30 two times more.

Cut off yarn A and change to yarn B.

Next round: *k13, place marker (using a different colour from the marker used to denote start of each round), rep from * to end. Change to DPN when work becomes too tight on circular needle.

Decreasing for crown

Next row: k2tog, *knit to 2 sts before marker, k2tog, slip marker, k2tog, rep from * four times, k to last 2 sts, k2tog [55 sts].

Repeat last round (decreasing 10 sts per round) until 25 sts remain.

Cut yarn and, using a needle, thread it through rem sts and draw them up tightly to fasten off.

Making up

Pull yarn up tightly and fasten off securely.

Cable-knit Bobble Hat

Materials:

3 balls of Aran (worsted/10-ply) alpaca/merino blend in light grey; 50g/94m/103yd

Needles:

7mm (UK 2, US 10½) needles

8mm (UK 0, US 11) needles

1 cable needle

Tension:

Tension over st st with single strand of yarn: 20 sts x 22 rows using 4.5mm (UK 7, US 7) needles

Instructions:

Using 7mm (UK 2, US 10½) needles and yarn doubled, cast on 74 sts.

Foundation row: knit each st through back loop to form a neat edge

Rows 1–9: *k1, p1, rep from * to end of row

Row 10: Work 1 x 1 rib as in rows 1–9 increasing 1 st in the middle of the row [75 sts].

Change to 8mm (UK 0, US 11) needles.

Main body

Cable and dot pattern

Row 1 (WS): *k2, k into front, back, front, back and front of next st (bobble made), k2, p2, k1, p2, k2, make bobble in next st as before, k2, rep from * to end.

Row 2: *p2, k5tog tbl (completing bobble), p2, C5F (sl 2 sts to cable needle and hold at front, k2, p1, k2 from cable needle), p2, k5tog tbl, p2, rep from * to end.

Row 3: *k5, p2, k1, p2, k5, rep from * to end.

Row 4: *p4, T3B (Twist 3 Back: slip next st onto cable needle and hold at back of work, knit 2, then purl st from cable needle), p1, T3F (Twist 3 Front: slip next 2 sts onto cable needle and hold at front of work, purl 1 then knit 2 from cable needle), p4, rep from * to end.

Row 5: *k4, p2, k3, p2, k4, rep from * to end.

Row 6: *p3, T3B, p3, T3F, p3, rep from * to end.

Row 7: *k3, p2, k2, make bobble in next st (as on first row), k2, p2, k3, rep from * to end.

Row 8: *p2, T3B, p2, k5tog tbl, p2, T3F, p2, rep from * to end.

Row 9: *k2, p2, k7, p2, k2, rep from * to end.

Row 10: *p1, T3B, p7, T3F, p1, rep from * to end.

Row 11: *k1, p2, k2, make bobble in next st, k3, make bobble in next st, k2, p2, k1, rep from * to end.

Row 12: *T3B, p2, k5tog tbl, p3, k5tog tbl, p2, T3F, rep from * to end.

Row 13: *p2, k11, p2, rep from * to end.

Row 14: *k2, p11, k2, rep from * to end.

Row 15: *p2, k3, make bobble in next st, k3, make bobble in next st, k3, p2, rep from * to end.

Row 16: *T3F, p2, k5tog tbl, p3, k5tog tbl, p2, T3B, rep from * to end.

Row 17: *k1, p2, k9, p2, k1, rep from * to end.

Row 18: *p1, T3F, p7, T3B, p1, rep from * to end.

Row 19: *k2, p2, k3, make bobble in next st, k3, p2, k2, rep from * to end.

Row 20: *p2, T3F, p2, k5tog tbl, p2, T3B, p2, rep from * to end.

Row 21: *k3, p2, k5, p2, k3, rep from * to end.

Row 22: *p3, T3F, p3, T3B, p3, rep from * to end.

Row 23: *k4, p2, k3, p2, k4, rep from * to end.

Row 24: *p4, T3F, p1, T3B, p4, rep from * to end.

Decreasing for crown

Row 25: k5, *p2tog, k1, p2tog, k4, k2tog, k4 rep from * to last 10 sts, p2tog, k1, p2tog, k5 [61 sts].

Row 26: p2, p2tog, p1, *k1, p1, k1, p2tog, p5, p2tog, rep from * to last 8 sts, k1,p1, k1, p2tog, p3 [51 sts].

Row 27: k1, *k3, k2tog, rep from * to end [41 sts].

Row 28: p1, *p2, p2tog, rep from * to end [31 sts].

Row 29: k1, *k1, k2tog, rep from * to end [21 sts].

Row 30: p1, *p2tog, rep from * to end [11 sts].

Making up

Cut yarn and thread through rem sts. Pull yarn up tightly and fasten off securely. Join back seam using mattress stitch.

Optional: Make one pompom and sew on top of hat.

Chunky Rainbow Knit

Materials:

5 balls of 100% chunky wool in blue (A), orange (B), mauve (C), yellow (D), white (E); 50g/43m/48yd

Needles:

1 pair of 4.5mm (UK 7, US 7) needles

1 pair of 5.5mm (UK 5, US 9) needles

Tension:

Tension over cable pattern: 14 sts x 18 rows using 5.5mm (UK 5, US 9) needles

Instructions:

Using 4.5mm (UK 7, US 7) needles and yarn A, cast on 87 sts.

Foundation row: knit each st through back loop to form a neat edge.

Rib row 1: *k2, p2, rep from * to last 3 sts, k2, p1.

Rib row 2: k1, p2, *k2, p2, rep from * to end.

Work rows 1 and 2 five more times.

Next row (RS): purl.

Next row (WS): k3, *kfb, k7, rep from * until last 4 sts, k4 [97 sts].

Change to yarn B and 5.5mm (UK 5, US 9) needles.

Main body

Cable pattern

Row 1 (RS): p2 *k6, p2, k6, p5; repeat from * to end.

Row 2 and all alt rows: knit the knit stitches and purl the purl stitches as they present themselves.

Row 3: p2, *work 6 st right crossover as follows: slip 4 sts to cable needle and hold at back of work, k2, k4 from cable needle, p2; work 6 st left crossover as follows: slip 2 sts to cable needle and hold at front of work, k4, k2 from cable needle, p5, rep from * to end.

Row 5: p2, *k4, work 3 st left crossover as follows: slip 2 sts to cable needle and hold in front, p1, k2 from cable needle: work 3 st right crossover as follows: slip 1 st to cable needle and hold at back of work, k2, p1 from cable needle, k4, p5, rep from * to end.

Row 7: p2, *k4, p1, work 4 st crossover as follows: slip 2 sts to cable needle and hold at front of work, k2, k2 from cable needle, p1, k4, p5, rep from * to end.

Row 9: p2, *k4, work 3 st right cross-over as follows: slip 1 st to cable needle and hold at back of work, k2, p1 from cable needle, work 3 st left cross-over as follows: slip 2 sts to cable needle and hold at front of work, p1, k2 from cable needle, k4, p5, rep from * to end.

Repeat rows 3–10 of cable pattern once using yarn C and once using yarn D.

Decreasing for crown

Change to yarn E.

Row 1: p2, *k2, k2tog, k2, p2, k2, k2tog, k2, p5 [87 sts].

Row 2: *k2, k2tog, k1, p2, p2tog, p1, k2tog, p2, p2tog, p1, rep from * to last 2 sts, k2tog [66 sts].

Row 3: p1, *k1, k2tog, k1, p1, k1, k2tog, k1, p1, p2tog, p1, rep from * to end [51 sts].

Row 4: *k2tog, k1, p2tog, p1, k1, p2tog, p1, rep from * to last st k1 [36 sts].

Row 5: p1, *k2tog, p1, k2tog, p2tog, rep from * to end [21 sts].

Making up

Cut yarn and thread through rem sts. Pull yarn up tightly and fasten off securely. Join back seam using mattress stitch.

Optional: Make one pompom using yarns B, C, D and E and sew on top of hat.

Fair Isle Tam

Materials:

4 balls of light DK (worsted/8-ply) alpaca yarn in sandstone (A), damson (B), rose (C), parchment (D); all 50g/112m/123yd

Needles:

1 pair of 3.75mm (UK 9, US 5) needles

1 pair of 4mm (UK 8, US 6) needles

1 cable needle

Tension:

Tension over Fair Isle pattern: 28 sts x 28 rows using 4mm (UK 8, US 6) needles

Instructions:

The pattern charts can be found on page 48.

Please check tension carefully before starting the hat.

Using 3.75mm (UK 9, US 5) needles and yarn A, cast on 112 sts.

Row 1 (RS): *k2, C4F, rep from * to last 4 sts, k4.

Row 2: Purl.

Row 3: Knit.

Row 4: Purl.

Rows 5 and 6: as rows 1 and 2.

Row 7: *C4B, k2 rep from * to end.

Row 8: Purl.

Rows 9 and 10: as rows 3 and 4.

Rows 11 and 12: as rows 7 and 8.

Row 13: k1, *M1, k2, rep from * to last st, M1, k1 [168 sts].

Row 14: Purl.

Change to 4mm needles.

Cut off yarn A.

Now work with yarn B (main) and yarn C.

Start working from row 1 of chart A, noting the odd-numbered rows are knitted and worked from right to left and the even-numbered rows are purled and worked from left to right. Continue working from chart until row 22.

Rows 23 and 24: st st yarn B.

Rows 25–32: as rows 1–8 of chart A (see page 48).

Decreasing for crown

Row 39: working in yarn A, *k10, k2tog tbl, k2tog, k10, rep from * 7 times [154 sts].

Row 40: purl [154 sts].

When decreasing for the crown in the following rows, follow Chart B and work RS (odd-numbered) rows by working section A once, then decreasing as instructed using appropriate colour, then working repeats of the main body followed by decreases as written on instruction rows and finally working section B.

When working the WS (even-numbered) rows, work section B once, purl 2 using appropriate colour, followed by repeats of the main body stitches as written on instruction rows, working final stitches from section A.

Row 41: *patt 9 sts, k2tog tbl, k2tog, patt 9 sts, rep from * 7 times [140 sts].

Row 42: *patt 9 sts, p2, patt 9 sts, rep from * 7 times

Row 43: *patt 8 sts, k2tog tbl, k2tog, patt 8 sts, rep from * 7 times [126 sts].

Row 44: *patt 8 sts, p2, patt 8 sts, rep from * 7 times

Row 45: *patt 7 sts, k2tog tbl, k2tog, patt 7 sts, rep from * 7 times [112 sts].

Row 46: *patt 7 sts, p2, patt 7 sts, rep from * 7 times

Row 47: *patt 6 sts, k2tog tbl, k2tog, patt 6 sts, rep from * 7 times [98 sts].

Row 48: *patt 6 sts, p2, patt 6 sts, rep from * 7 times

Row 49: *patt 5 sts, k2tog tbl, k2tog, patt 5 sts, rep from * 7 times [84 sts].

Row 50: *patt 5 sts, p2, patt 5 sts, rep from * 7 times

Row 51: *patt 4 sts, k2tog tbl, k2tog, patt 4, rep from * 7 times [70 sts].

Row 52: *patt 4 sts, p2, patt 4 sts, rep from * 7 times

Row 53: *patt 3 sts, k2tog tbl, k2tog, patt 3 sts, rep from * 7 times [56 sts].

Row 54: *patt 3 sts, p2, patt 3 sts, rep from * 7 times

Row 55: *patt 2 sts, k2tog tbl, k2tog, patt 2 sts, rep from * 7 times [42 sts].

Row 56: *patt 2 sts, p2, patt 2 sts, rep from * 7 times

Row 57: *patt 1 st, k2tog tbl, k2tog, patt 1 st, rep from * 7 times [28 sts].

Row 58: *patt 1 st, p2, patt 1 st, rep from * 7 times

Row 59: using yarn A, *k2tog tbl, k2tog, rep from * to end [14 sts].

Row 60: *p2tog, rep from * to end [7 sts].

Cut yarn and thread through remaining stitches. Pull up yarn tightly and fasten off securely.

Making up

Sew up side seams using mattress stitch. Weave in loose ends to WS of work.

Make a short i-cord in yarn A and sew it onto the top of your tam.

Fair Isle Beanie

Materials:

4 balls of 4-ply (fingering) baby alpaca/silk blend in French navy (A), parchment (B), coral (C), forget-me-not (D); 50g/225m/246yd

Needles:

3.25mm (UK 10, US 3) circular knitting needles, 40cm (16in)

3.25mm (UK 10, US 3) DPN

Tension square:

32 sts x 35 rows = 10cm (4in) over Fair Isle pattern using 3.25mm (UK 10, US 3) circular needles

Instructions:

Using the circular needles, cast on 128 sts in yarn A. Place a stitch marker to denote start of each round. Join the round being careful not to twist any stitches. Slip marker as you pass it on every round.

Rounds 1–8: using A, *k1, p1, rep from * to end of round.

Next round: *k3, inc in next stitch, rep from * to end [160 sts].

Next 3 rounds: work from chart A.

Chart A

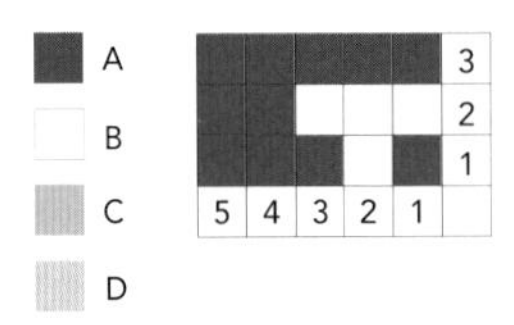

Next round: using yarn A, *k9, kfb in next stitch, rep from * to end [176 sts].

Next 13 rounds: work from chart B.

Chart B

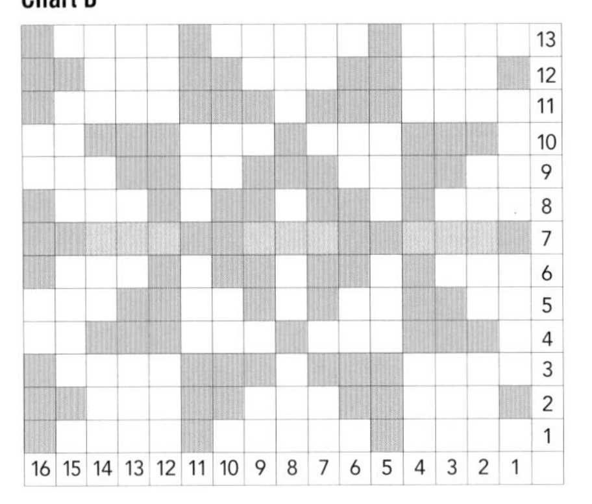

Next round: using yarn A, *k10 inc in next stitch, rep from * to end [192 sts].

Next round: Using yarn B, increase 3 sts evenly across round [195 sts].

Next 9 rounds: work from chart C.

Chart C

Next round: using yarn B, decrease 3 stitches evenly across the row [192 sts].

Next round: using yarn A, *k4, k2tog, rep from * to end [160 sts].

Next 9 rounds: work from Chart D.

Chart D

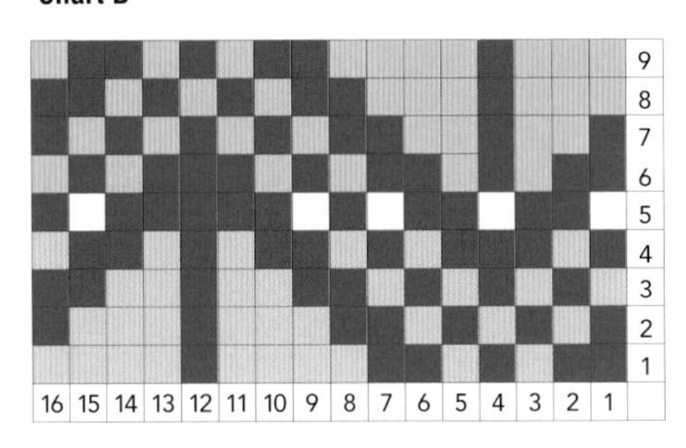

Next round: using yarn A, *k3, k2tog, rep from * to end [128 sts].

Next 4 rounds: work from Chart E. Note that for the last 3 sts, you knit the first 3 sts from the chart.

Chart E

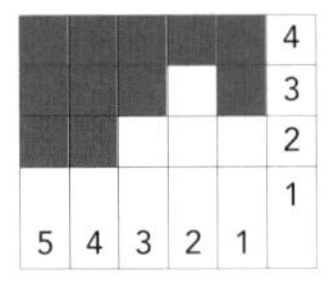

Now distribute your stitches evenly across 4 DPN.

Next round: k4, *k2, k2tog, rep from * to last 4 sts, k4 [98 sts].

Next three rounds: work as rounds 4–6 from chart C, from chart C, reversing colours and noting the round finishes on the first stitch from the chart. On the third round inc 2 sts [100 sts].

Work 4 rounds from Chart F; when you reach **xxx** work sl1, k2tog, psso over those 3 sts [90 sts].

Chart F

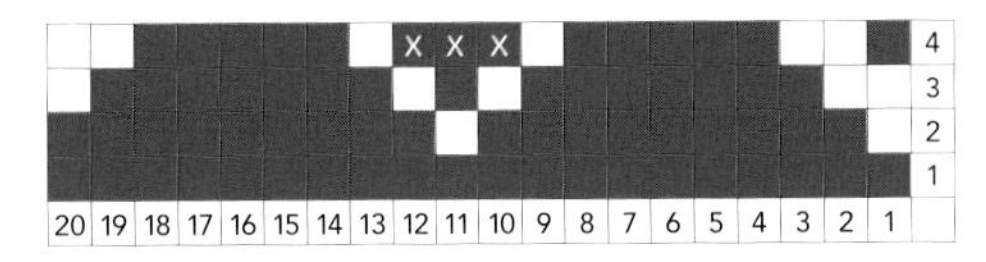

Next 2 rounds: work from Chart G decreasing as above for **xxx** [80 sts].

Chart G

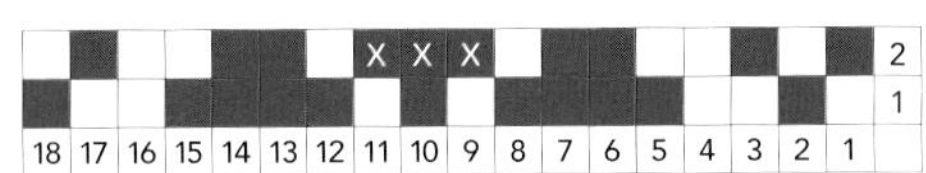

Next round: knit using yarn A.

Next round: *k7, sl 1, k2tog, psso, k6, rep to end [70 sts].

Next round: *k4D, k3C, rep from * to end.

Next round: *k4D, k3C, Sl 1, k2tog, psso, k1 (all D), k3C, rep from * to end [60 sts].

Next round: knit each stitch as it appears in the same colours as the previous row.

Next round: using yarn B, *k4, sl1, k2tog, psso, k5, rep from to * to end [50 sts].

Next round: using yarn B, knit.

Next round: using yarn B, *k3, sl1, k2tog, psso, k4, rep from to * to end [40 sts].

Next round: using yarn B, *k2, sl1, k2tog, psso, k3, rep from * to end [30 sts].

Next round: *sl1, k2tog, psso, rep from to * to end [10 sts].

Making up

Cut yarn and thread through rem sts. Pull yarn up tightly and fasten off. Weave in all loose ends.

Peruvian-style hat

Materials:

3 balls of Aran (worsted/10-ply) in rooster (A), deep sea (B), custard (C); 50g/93m/103yd

Needles:

4.5 mm (UK 7, US 7) needles

5mm (UK 6, US 8) needles

Large-eyed tapestry needle

Tension:

Tension over Fair Isle: 20 sts x 22 rows using 5mm (UK 6, US 8) needles

Instructions:

Ear flaps (make two identical flaps)

Cast on 3 stitches in yarn A using the 5mm (US 8, UK 6) needles.

Row 1 (WS): knit.

Row 2 (RS): knit into the front and back of each stitch [6 sts].

Rows 3 and 4: as rows 1 and 2 [12 sts].

Row 5: k4, p4, k4.

Row 6: k4, kfb, k2, kfb, k4 [14 sts].

Row 7: k4, p6, k4.

Row 8: k4, kfb, k4, kfb, k4 [16 sts].

Row 9: k4, p8, k4.

Row 10: Knit.

Repeat rows 9 and 10, five more times.

Set aside.

Main body

Next row (WS): cast on 15 sts in yarn A, work k4, p8, k4 across WS of first ear flap, cast on 38 sts in yarn A, work k4, p8, k4 across WS of second earflap, cast on 15 sts in yarn A [100 sts].

Next row (RS): k15 through the back loop, k16, k38 through the back loop, k16, k15 through the back loop.

Purl 1 row.

Now work the 5 rows from Chart A, noting that the pattern is repeated 6 times across the row and then the first 10 sts are repeated once more. Note when working Fair Isle the odd-numbered rows are read from right to left (knit rows) and for even-numbered rows the chart is read from left to right (purl rows). Remember to begin WS row on same st previous RS row ended on.

Chart A

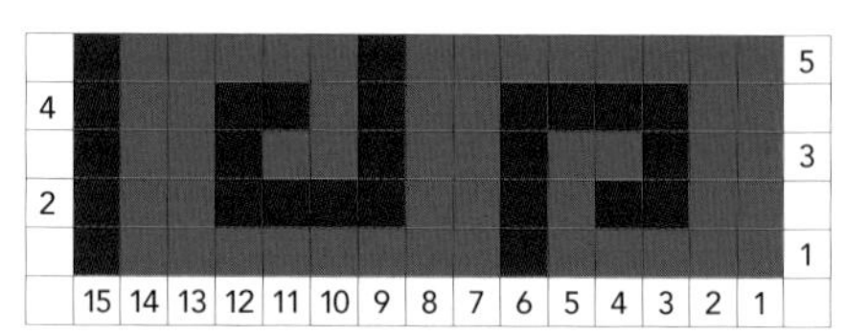

Row 6: using yarn A, purl.

Rows 7 and 8: using yarn A, knit.

Row 9: using yarn C, knit.

Row 10: using yarn C, purl.

Rows 11–21: work from chart B.

Chart B

A C

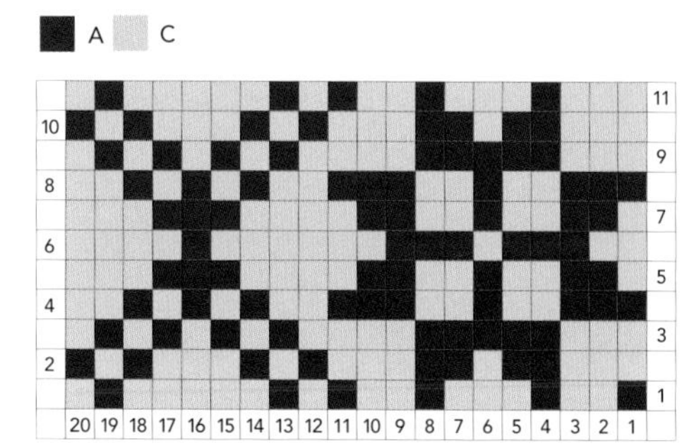

Row 22: using yarn C, purl.

Rows 23 and 24: using yarn C, knit.

Rows 25 and 26: using yarn B, work 2 rows in st st.

Rows 27–33: work from chart C.

Chart C

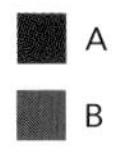

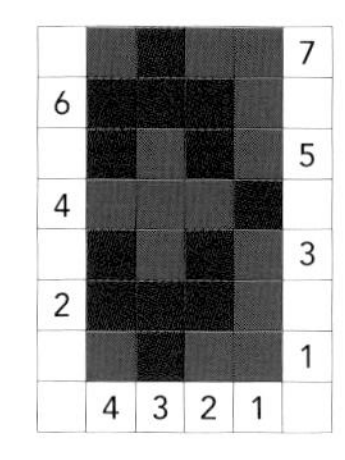

Row 34: using yarn B, purl.

Rows 35 and 36: using yarn B, knit.

Row 37: *k2A, k2C, rep from * to end.

Row 38: *p2C, p2A, rep from * to end.

Row 39: *k2C, k2A, rep from * to end.

Row 40: *p2A, p2C, rep from * to end.

Row 41: using yarn B, *k1, sl 1, k1, psso, rep from * to last st, k1 [67 sts].

Row 42: using yarn B, knit.

Row 43: as row 41 [45 sts].

Row 44: using yarn B, purl.

Row 45: *k1, sl 1, k1, psso, rep from * to end [30 sts].

Row 46: Purl.

Row 47:*k2tog, rep from * to end [15 sts].

Thread a needle through sts leaving a long tail end for sewing up.

Hat border

Using yarn A and 4.5mm knitting needle and with RS of work facing you, pick up and knit 12 sts from straight edge, 28 sts around first ear flap, 30 sts from long straight edge, 28 sts around second ear flap and 12 sts from final straight edge [110 sts].

Cast off all stitches on your needle.

Making up

Pull yarn up tightly at the top of the hat and fasten off securely. Join back seam using a mattress stitch. Weave in strands of yarn.

Make two plaits approx. 38cm (15in) long, using yarn A, and attach to bottom points of ear flaps.

Striped-rim Fair Isle

Materials:

6 balls of 4-ply Shetland yarn in dark grey (A), light blue (B), light grey (C), variegated heather pink (D), light pink (E), natural white (F); 25g/105m/114yd

Needles:

3mm (UK 11, US 2½) needles

Tension:

Tension over Fair Isle: 28 sts x 30 rows using 3mm (UK 11, US 2½) needles

Instructions:

The pattern chart can be found on page 48.

Using 3mm (UK 11, US 2½) needles and yarn A, cast on 120 sts.

Foundation row: knit each st through back loop to form a neat edge.

Rows 1 and 2: using yarn B, knit.

Rows 3 and 4: using yarn B, *k2, p2, rep from * to end.

Rows 5–8: as rows 1–4 in yarn A.

Rows 9–24: Repeat rows 1–8 two more times.

Cut off yarn B. Start working from chart row 1 and, on this row only: k3, M1, *k6, M1, rep from * to last 3 sts, k3 [140 sts].

Continue working from chart until all 36 rows have been worked.

Decreasing for crown

Row 1: *k2A, k2C, k6A, k1C, k6A, k2C, k1A, rep from * to end.

Row 2: *p4C, p4A, s2ppC, p4A, p4C, p1A, rep from * to end [126 sts].

Row 3: *k2C, k1A, k2C, k2A, k2C, k1A, k2C, k2A, k2C, k1A, k1C, rep from * to end.

Row 4: *p1A, p3B, p2A, p1B, S2ppB, p1B, p2A, p3B, p1A, p1B, rep from * to end [112 sts].

Row 5: *k1A, k3B, k2A, k2B, k1A, k2B, k2A, k3B, rep from * to end.

Row 6: *p2B, p3A, p1B, s2ppB, p1B, p3A, p3B, rep from * to end [98 sts].

Row 7: *k2B, k3A, k2B, k1A, k2B, k3A, k1B, rep from * to end.

Row 8: *p4A, p1B, s2ppB, p1B, p4A, p1B, rep from * to end [84 sts].

Row 9: *k1B, k3A, k2B, k1A, k2B, k3A, rep from * to end.

Row 10: *p3A, p1B, s2ppB, p1B, p3A, p1B, rep from * to end [70 sts].

Row 11: *k1B, k2A, k2B, k1A, k2B, k2A, rep from * to end.

Row 12: *p2A, p1C, S2ppC, p1C, p2A, p1C, rep from * to end [56 sts].

Row 13: *k2A, k2C, k1A, k2C, k1A, rep from * to end.

Row 14: *p1A, p1C, s2ppC, p1C, p2A, rep from * to end [42 sts].

Row 15: *k1A, k2C, k1A, k2C, rep from * to end.

Row 16: *p1B, s2ppB, p1B, p1A, rep from * to end [28 sts].

Row 17: *k2B, k1A, k1B, rep from * to end.

Row 18: *s2ppC, k1A, rep from * to end [14 sts].

Making up

Cut yarn and thread through remaining stitches. Pull yarn up tightly and fasten off securely. Join back seam using mattress stitch.

Patterns

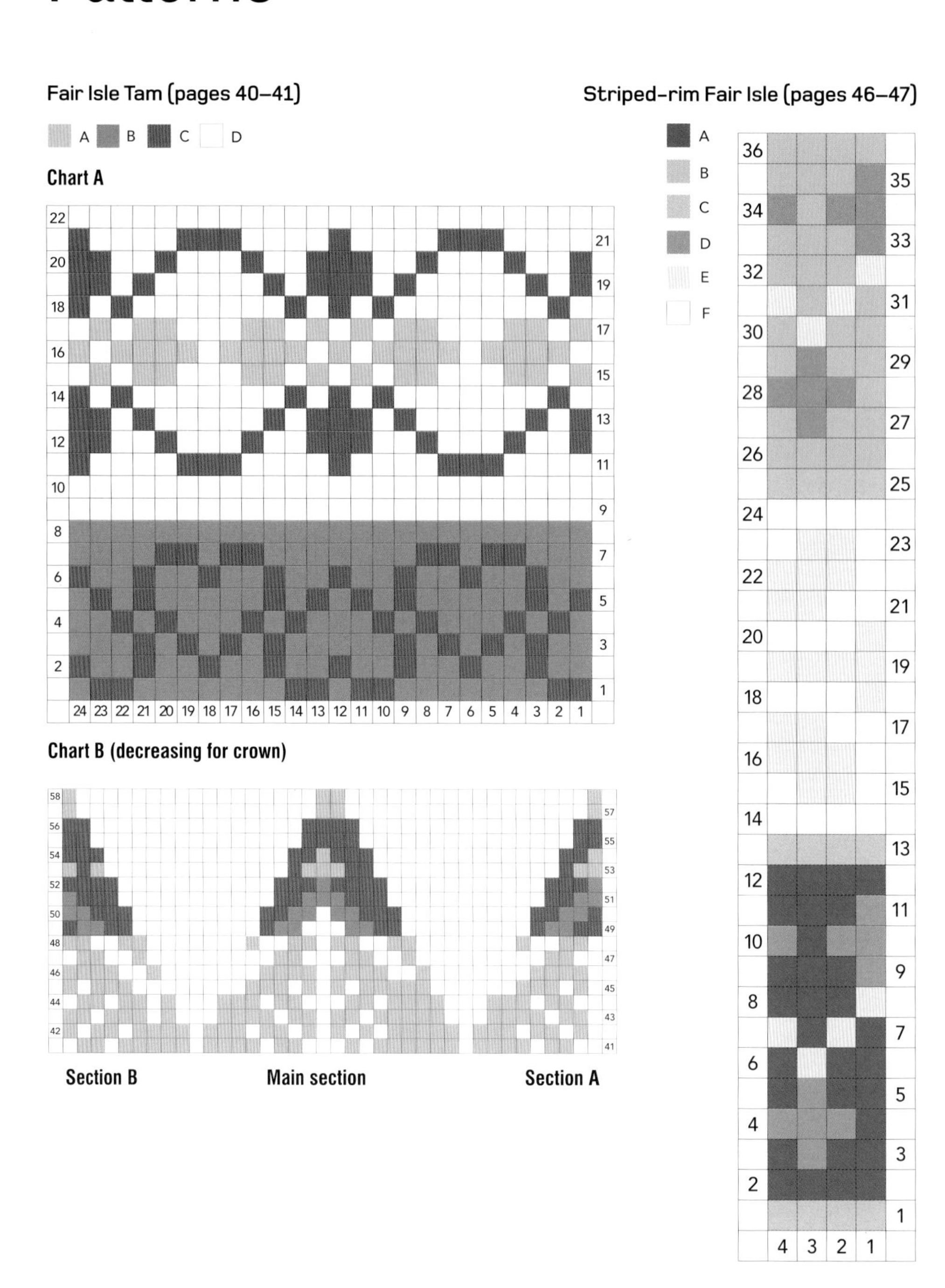

Fair Isle Tam (pages 40–41)
A
B
C
D
Chart A
22
21
20
19
18
17
16
15
14
13
12
11
10
9
8
7
6
5
4
3
2
1
24 23 22 21 20 19 18 17 16 15 14 13 12 11 10 9 8 7 6 5 4 3 2 1
Chart B (decreasing for crown)
58
57
56
55
54
53
52
51
50
49
48
47
46
45
44
43
42
41
Section B
Main section
Section A
Striped-rim Fair Isle (pages 46–47)
A
B
C
D
E
F
36
35
34
33
32
31
30
29
28
27
26
25
24
23
22
21
20
19
18
17
16
15
14
13
12
11
10
9
8
7
6
5
4
3
2
1
4 3 2 1